BERNARD QUARM

CAREER PATH

The Pursuit of Purpose

'The future isn't a place that we are going; it is a place that we get to create'.

– Nancy Durate, communication expert

BERNARD QUARM

CAREER PATH

The Pursuit of Purpose

For Students, Graduates, New Employees and All

Career Path
The Pursuit of Purpose

Cover design by Exceller Books using resources from Pixabay.com

ISBN: 978-93-93734-76-1

First published in India in 2023 by Exceller Books
An Imprint of GE Group

Address: G1, Dream Apartment, Degree College Road, Belgharia, Kolkata, 700056, India

www.excellerbooks.com

Dear reader,

One of the greatest gifts and treasures of life is knowledge – illumination. It is said that what you have no knowledge about has an advantage over you. I have, therefore, come to the conclusion that no one is greater than their level of knowledge. One of the critical and yet silent killers of this era is ignorance.

'The power of the oppressor is in the maintenance of ignorance.'Dr. Myles Monroe

The paradox of our generation is that, despite the abundance of information and discoveries, there seems to be a high display of folly and ignorance. Ignorance has destroyed many lives, shattered the dreams and aspirations of many, and given rise to truncated hopes and visions.

Ignorance, first emerging from our homes, has spread over societies and communities, crossed international boundaries, and affected a large number of people. I am, therefore, right to list ignorance as a pandemic. It is worth noting that the antidote to this epidemic is knowledge, which produces illumination and brings understanding. Knowledge has the power to transform the mind. Knowledge is the light that gives insight, and this light is mostly planted in books. It is, therefore, imperative that one cultivates the culture of reading.

No one is indeed greater than their reading life; anyone who aspires to lead must read. An individual's strength lies in what they are exposed to or have knowledge of. Besides books, this knowledge is also stored in magazines, encyclopedia, and most contemporary digital search engines like Google, Bing, Yahoo, etc. It is not enough to cultivate a culture of reading, there is a need to have the intelligence to know what to read because our lives reflect what we read and know.

Reading is a solitary act. For many of us, it is a form of retreat – a welcomed silence and deserved rest from demanding routines. We have our favourite spot in the house – the bed unmade, the couch long enough to doze on, or maybe the off-limits living room. Wherever it is, when we are there with the book in hand and maybe our favourite cup of tea (mine is Indian tea), all who encounter us know they have to 'shush' because it is reading time. The greatest legacy we can give to the younger generation (the future unseen) is to expose them radically to the habit and culture of reading, reading quality, and productive materials. An informed citizenry is a nation's heritage and wealth. I want to encourage individuals, institutions, and nations at large to adopt and intensify the culture of reading and apply them for maximum impact.

Join the LUPCONSULT *Elite Club* today!

Dedication

I dedicate this informative resource to the teens and youth in Ghana and the rest of the world. Young people are the messages we send to the future we may not feature in.

Acknowledgment

Every book requires the toil, time, and devotion of extraordinary people who may be directly or indirectly connected to you. Words will be inadequate to express my gratitude to the people God assigned to work with me on this tremendous project – Career Path.

Though I fear making the mistake of leaving some of them out, I do want to acknowledge the great effort of the following people:

My father, Rev Solomon Quarm, who has been an immense source of inspiration and support to me,

Hon. Christopher Neyor and Ms. Saalai Manikam, whose examples as mentors are unrivalled, propelled my desire to write this book.

Special thanks go to Very Rev Kwasi A. Sakyi- Appiah the former Minister in charge, Christ the King Methodist church, East Legon – Accra and Prophet Darko Mensah and his family for their genuine care and encouragement.

I want to specially express my heartfelt appreciation to Dr. David Mensah, Miss Nasiba Bawa, Lawyer Ama Dzifa Amankwah, Kay, Mr. Ebo Bhavnani, Angelina, Priscilla, and Akosua, who spent precious moments of their time reading through the script and making the necessary corrections. To all who, in diverse ways, supported this great work, thank you, and God bless you.

Table of Contents

Foreword

I would like to introduce Mr. Bernard Quarm, affectionately called Ben Quarm's new book titled *Career Path – the Pursuit of Purpose*. With tremendous enthusiasm and also as an educationist, I highly recommend this book to you.

I see Ben Quarm, as an emerging world-class leader who believes in intentional and transformative servant leadership. His ideas and ideals about education, and leadership are unique as they embed a dimension of practical and result-driven principles. His thoughts about Career, Education, and Capacity development revealed in this book are breathtaking and unique. Career Path gives the reader in-depth knowledge about themselves, the system in which they operate, and how to choose a career trajectory that reveals one's intrinsic worth.

I am intrigued by his depth of knowledge and revelations in this book. Career Path will clear certain myths and doubts and show you the way to live a successful life as far as your career is concerned. I implore all students, educational institutions, and all to lay hold of this masterpiece.

Eugene K. M. Dartey – Ph.D,
Board Chairman –National Schools Inspectorate Authority,
NaSIA
Accra, Ghana

Commendations

This is a good resource for all who are about to enter the job market, those already in it but seeking a new challenge, and the employed who are not realizing their career dreams. This book will help readers to refocus, maximize their potential and achieve the fulfillment they desire to achieve in their chosen careers. I recommend this book to graduates, the newly employed, and those who believe they have reached the pinnacle of their careers. To the last group, this will help you self-evaluate.

Ama Dzifa Amankwah Esi
LLB, LLM, BL
Director for System Reform International Justice Missions
Ghana

If I had access to resourceful material such as this during my secondary and tertiary education, I would have made more informed decisions about my career. Nonetheless, it has never been late as I have learned a lot from reading this book, and without reservation, say "Career Path" is a timely resource for this generation, especially those who wish to excel as far as their career is concerned. This book is, by all standards, a useful resource, and I recommend it to all, especially students, graduates, and new employees.

Charlotte Dadzie
BSc. Agric. Biotechnology
Kwame Nkrumah University of Science and Technology
(KNUST) Ghana

Career Path is a great resource for anyone seeking to develop their competencies and seeking to make a mark in their career choice. I recommend this work to every young person.

Rt. Rev. Moses Owusu-Sekyere
Bishop – Word of Faith Missions, UK

Blessed be the Lord who has given you this blueprint for Career Development. I have read many books concerning careers, but I am intrigued by the direction and thoughts embedded in this book. Indeed, our Career choices must reflect our intrinsic worth – our purpose! I enjoyed reading this book, and I agree with most of the information written in it. I hope to see the youth practice the lessons in this book because, from personal experience, I can tell the kind of fruits there are in putting such elucidating thoughts to practice. Against this backdrop, I recommend this piece to anyone who wishes to maximize their potential, especially tertiary and senior High students.

Edwin Asa Adjei
Editorial Assistant, CIHA blog (Critical Investigations intoHumanitarianism in Africa) www.cihablog.com

In making a journey to a destination that one has never been before, one needs direction. This direction on our highways is provided on directional signposts as one drives along. There is that which everybody needs in order to get to his or her destination as far as career is concerned. All these nuggets, which I call directional signs, have been professionally provided by Mr. Bernard Quarm in this all-important book. This is a contemporary piece that the youth of our day need very much. I strongly recommend this to every school-going youth as well as those about to join the career populace within and outside Ghana. Take this piece with you as a textbook as you travel along your career path, and you will surely arrive safely.

David Y. Mensah (Ph.D.)
Statistician, Researcher & Career Coach,
Accra- Ghana

In this fluctuating and uncertain economy, the job market is more competitive than ever, and to live effectively, it is imperative that you strategically market yourself – your core competencies. Bernard Quarm, having exhibited this practical truth, has revealed the secret in this book. He talks about the fact that without a solid brand and good packaging, it will be difficult to attract the attention of employers. I believe by this masterpiece, the rich secret of making a difference in your world will be unravelled.

Christopher Neyor
New York, United States

Introduction

Some books are difficult to write; others border on the almost impossible, and this one is in the latter category. Many thoughts and ideas, coupled with suggestions and advice from friends and even strangers over the years, threw me into a state of indecision. Moreover, the pain, confusion, and gloomy picture of the future, which kept coming to mind, got me thinking. There I concluded the time had come to write this piece – the fundamental nugget for career success. Picking inspiration from the words of Dr. Samuel Koranteng Pipim and Dr. Joyce Aryee from their book – The Transformed Mind, I was encouraged to put together this masterpiece. A book that will serve as a blueprint for earthly success and eternal achievement. Our world today houses many who are confused and are at a crossroads in their lives in terms of life choices and decisions. Others live with the pain and hurt of the decisions they made in the past, born out of wrong choices. Most of the time, this situation, in which many find themselves, is a result of ignorance, lack of counsel, and misplaced priorities. The foundation on which these issues stem from is that many people do not have adequate knowledge of who they are (identity crisis) and the environment in which they live (nurture). When a person does not have adequate information about who they really are, it gives others the right to tell them who they are not.

Again, our world fails woefully with an unhealthy mix of the unintelligent and shoddy and the intelligent but arrogant. We seem to amass so much knowledge and titles, yet nobody gets the work done.

Introduction

The youth today are thrown off balance as far as their career and self-discovery are concerned, with social media becoming their demi-god. They go through the systems and structures put in place as a means of enlightenment but end up not having the slightest idea of what they really want to do with their lives. Those who come to know are confronted with so many challenges, with finance being the key factor to these challenges. These are the exact words of a graduate with a second class (Upper honours) I met during my research moments – he was an Uber driver.

> 'If I knew I would go to school only to end up being an Uber driver because there are no jobs, I would have invested all those monies and time spent in acquiring a degree certificate in a profitable venture.'

This is not to say being an Uber driver is a bad idea, but the fact that what he studied has no connection with what he is doing seems quite frustrating. Education which is supposed to bring enlightenment and mass economic growth, is now the reasonfor increased corruption, war, and greed. "While earlier textbooks for young children started teaching simple arithmetic by asking pupils to count donkeys, they are currently counting Kalashnikovs (Ak47) – children are being prepared for war instead of life'.

> 'It is the supreme art of the teacher to awaken joy in creative expression, knowledge, and performance management.' – Albert Einstein

The teacher, to awaken the joy of creativity, must himor herself be creative enough. The economic and leadership worlds today are clear reflections of what we have been taught in school. An educational system or structure is supposed to help learners to discover their unique career paths and assist them in developing their 'calling' in order to rightly fit into the world by bringing solutions to unending challenges.

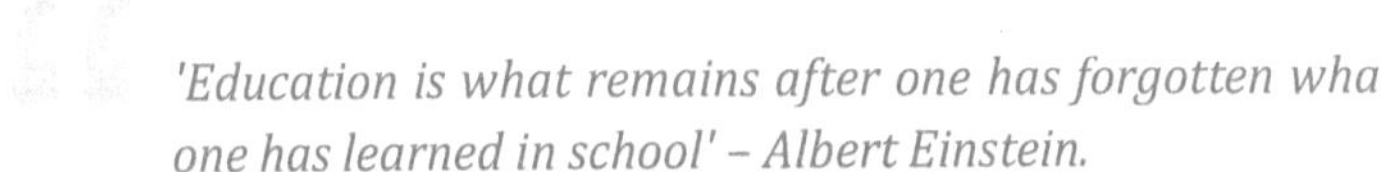

'Education is what remains after one has forgotten what one has learned in school' – Albert Einstein.

Education is a lot more than just what happens in a classroom. It is possible to go through school without being properly educated. Education is deeper and has far-reaching ramifications on society and the mindset of the educated individual. As social beings, we interact with our environment, which leads us to discovery and knowledge of ourselves and the things around us. We do not expect to use yesterday's knowledge to combat issues of today, hence the need to explore and give room for continuous development.

'Education is not knowledge; it provides a platform to acquire knowledge. Through education, we acquire knowledge" – Ms. Saalai Manikam.

Again, education should be able to reveal each person's abilities and present a clear map of people's ambitions and passions. It should, at the end of the day, build the individual intellectually, morally, and innovatively as a social change agent for national development. The content and context of education really matter. D.L Moody had it right when he said, "If you educate a thief who steals bolts and knots from the rail station will steal the whole railway when he graduates". Curriculum developers must take into critical account the content of the materials used for intellectual discourse. We must give thought to the content of what it is that we seek to use as a subject matter for education.

They must seek to embrace content that can bring about a visible transformation in the lives of people and the nations of the world. I trust that the principles in this book will help you in achieving the purpose for which you decided to buy it. In order to experience this change that I have discussed in this book, I suggest you follow the principles outlined below:

- ✓ Have an in-depth desire for change. Change begins with us, and it must start with a decision to become a person of value.
- ✓ Use the skimming method to read through the entire book to understand the direction, or idea that the book promotes.
- ✓ After this, take your time and read through the book chapter by chapter thoroughly and apply them at every point of your life.
- ✓ Evaluate yourself to see whether you are being transformed by the principles. If not, check whether you are applying the principles accordingly.

I encourage you to share these principles with friends and loved ones to liberate them from the bondage of graduate unemployment. May the Heavens graciously grant you understanding, wisdom, and motivation to identify, pursue and establish that which God has planned for you. Read on!

Bernard Quarm
Director, LUPCONSULT LTD
quarmbernard@yahoo.com

1|Overview of Today's Job Market

The Job Market – Then and Now

The job market is a business concept in which employers search for employees and employees search for jobs. It is not a physical place, much as it is a concept demonstrating the competition and interplay between different labour forces. The job market, also known as the labour market, can grow or shrink depending on the demand for labour and the availability of workers within the overall economy. Several factors determine the state of the labour market. These include; the needs of a specific industry, the need for a particular educational level or skill set, and required job functions. The job market is a significant component of any economy and is directly tied to the demand for goods and services. It is important to note that the interplay between the needs of industries and the accompanying educational level or skills required to meet that specific need determines how the job market operates.

The job market takes different forms and dimensions at every point in time. For example, the Job market of the 18th century is different from that of the 21st century. The 18th century was a period of intellectual, social, and political ferment known as the Age of Enlightenment. Under this revolution, machines, techniques, and new skills rapidly replaced manual work. It started in Britain and then spread to the rest of the world. It was the age of mass production that gave birth to many business owners. As a result, there was a rise in employment opportunities with very little trained or skilled labour. This made employers take advantage of the existing situation by paying employees meagre salaries. During this era, men mostly dominated the labour market as most of the women did not have formal education and were confined to their homes.

In contrast, the 21st-century job market is sophisticated, because the industrial revolution has taken another dimension due to technological advancement. In this age, not only do we have qualified labour force chasing after limited and sometimes non-existing jobs, but also technology has replaced many workers. It is essential to note that, as automation and artificial intelligence technologies improve, there will be millions of people laid off, which poses great anxiety to the labour market. Despite this challenge, one economist argued;

> *'Since the dawn of the industrial age, a recurrent fear has been that technological change will spawn mass unemployment. A neoclassical economist, on the other hand, predicted that this would not happen because people would develop or find other jobs, albeit possibly after a long period of painful adjustment.*

In summary, the job market in the 18th century was characterized by the industrial revolution whiles the 21st-century job market presents a more challenging situation where seeking jobs in certain industries will be difficult or require a high level of technical skill.

The job market is directly related to the unemployment rate. Theunemployment rate is the percentage of people in the labour force who are currently unemployed but are available and actively seeking a job. The higher the unemployment rate, the greater the supply of labour in the overall job market. When employers have a large pool of applicants to choose from, they can be selective or can reduce wages. Conversely, as the unemployment rate drops, employers are forced to compete for the few available workers. The competition for workers has the effect of increasing wages. Wages determined by the job market provide valuable information for economic analysts and those who set public policies based on the health of the overall economy. During difficult economic times, unemployment tends to rise.

A clear example is the year 2020 when there was a record of the highest level of layoffs by employers due to the Corona Virus pandemic. Employers are forced to lay off some workers creating fewer jobs, hence making it difficult for people to land a job. This is a clear picture of the 21st-century job market. High rates of unemployment can prolong economic stagnation [a sustained period of little to no growth in an economy] and contribute to social upheaval, leading to the loss of opportunities for many individuals to live comfortably.

The 21st-century job market is filled with a high rate of unemployment – this issue is not a result of the absence of jobs, but then the absence of soft and employability skills such as communication, attitude, critical thinking, etc. Much of this challenge could be blamed on the education system, including higher education institutions which are not keeping up with the needs of the job market.

Preparing for the 21st-century Job Market

In today's job market, employers want to hire and work with versatile people who have a variety of these 21st-century skill sets. They also want to see a record of continual learning achievement and a digital portfolio that demonstrates competence, creativity, and forward-thinking. There is no better way to develop a 21st-century career than harnessing the incredible power of self-directed online learning, volunteering, and undergoing professional development. When you can learn independently and apply what you learn by building your own creative projects, you thrive in a world of accelerated change.

To create a social element for your self-directed learning, I recommend seeking out other self-directed learners in your area and organizing study and mastermind groups where you can schedule weekly virtual meetings using online collaboration tools like Google Hangouts, Zoom, Microsoft Teams, etc. You can also meet at local coffee shops or join a co-working space. The most fundamental skill for the 21st-century career is how you tell your story and turn your ideas into reality. In the 21st century, you have everything you need at your fingertips to actively develop your knowledge and skills through self-directed learning, and that is what makes the future so exciting and full of possibilities.

The 3 L's of the 21st Century Job Market

In addition to the above, it is very important to learn how to unlearn old ways of doing things, relearn what you have not mastered, and learn new skills in order to place you in a leading situation. There are scores of skill sets needed for the 21st-century job market. I will discuss three core skills that are very important to one's career success. The 3 L's are the broad skill set needed to be relevant and strategically positioned in the 21st-century job market. The first L stands for Learning Skills, the second L is Literacy Skills, and the final L stands for Life Skills.

Learning Skills:

Learning skills involve how we process information and connect the dots between different subjects. It also involves developing our ability to collaborate and communicate the values of our ideas in a clear and concise way. This skill engages critical thinking, creative thinking, collaboration, and communication.

Literacy Skills:

Literacy skills involve how we recognise truth from fiction on socialmedia networks on the web. It is knowing how to use information technology to share your stories and inspire people. This skill is not taught; it is caught. Students, especially graduates, must be conscious of this and act accordingly. The Literacy skill also engages information literacy, media literacy, and technology literacy.

Life Skills:

Life skills deal with the ability of taking initiatives, creating a vision for yourcareer, and developing your personal brand. We all need to work on being more confident leaders who get things done. This skill requires flexibility, initiatives, social skills, productivity, and leadership skills. Join the level – up conference to enjoy a more practical stimulating experience.

When an advertisement for a position in a reputable organization is published, one of the things every graduate should note is that he or she is competing with over 1000 other candidates in a highly competitive job market. There could be instances where applicants are fewer and instances where they are even more. As noted earlier, the current job market nowadays is choked and highly competitive. It is not like in the 18th century when employers would come to mount up their companies' stands at graduation ceremonies of universities to scramble for enterprising and promising students and graduates. Even though it is still ongoing, its relevance is almost outlived.

> *It was employers chasing after qualified graduates, and each graduate could at least be assured of a job. But now, what do we see today? The tables have turned against the graduates. We are now chasing jobs, sometimes non-existing jobs.*

Statistically, about 520,000 plus people enter the labour market in Ghana every year. These individuals graduate from universities, polytechnics, and technical and vocational institutions, including high schools as well as apprenticeship schools. Out of this, about 12,000 to 15,000 graduates, i.e., those with specific government placement allocation (Teachers, Doctors, Nurses, etc.), are absorbed by government institutions through the Controller and Accountant General's department, which places these individuals on the government's payroll. As a result of this, the majority of job seekers (graduates) have instinctively turned their attention to private organizations and entrepreneurship in order to survive. The net effect is an excess supply of graduates and a spate of underemployment. The is indeed the reason the Ghanaian Educational curricula must be considered as far as their revision is concerned to equip students with the necessary skills to reduce structural unemployment. In addition, students should also take the responsibility to train and empower themselves with practical, employable skills to be of great benefit to their community.

'See a man diligent in his work; he shall stand before princes and kings.' We need men and women of integrity who are humble and responsible.

Student-graduates must then be wise to equip themselves with workable theoretical and practical skills, which will at least increase their chances of getting a job. As a student, you need to be intentional and knowledgeable about what you really want out of life. This is actually the secret to experiencing a life of fulfilment; when you are able to know who you are and what exactly you are born to deliver, it is almost like killing two birds with one stone. As it is with individuals, so is it with nations. Policies, projects, and investments must sync with what we seek or desire to achieve out of life for the citizens of every nation.

At LUP Consult, this is what we seek to achieve; to present a worldview of possibilities and mass enlightenment by developing quality labour force. Do not be left out in our annual flagship programme – level up the conference. Register to join.

2|The Blueprint of the Career World

All About Career – Career Explained

'Everyone has a calling. And your real job in life is to figure out as soon as possible what that is, who you were meant to be and begin to honor that in the best way possible for yourself' – Oprah Winfrey

The most predominant question the young graduate or student is asked is; "What do you wish to be in the future?", "What do you want to be when you grow up?" etc. Many youngsters mention ambitious careers without considering the factors and consequences of a career choice. Others, for the fun of it, wish to be something they do not have the slightest idea about. This question seems very simple but confusing and sometimes difficult to answer, not because we do not understand what it means. Largely the confusion is because we want to be many things. In some cases, the desires of others can influence us to become what we do not desire or wish to become. Therefore, we end up saying things that frustrate us because we cannot realize them. You will not be able to choose or identify a career that will grant you earthly satisfaction and eternal accomplishment until you discover your identity and your purpose.

Self-identity – who you are is the fundamental question that leads to career discovery.

This chapter elaborates on what a career is all about and helps you identify who you are, so you will know the career which best fits you. The curriculum of every nation must be driven towards helping students to, first of all, know who they are, i.e., their purpose, passion, desire, ambition, etc., and second, help them to unearth their potential. There are many theories, definitions, and ideas about career that underscores the worldview of those who propounded these theories or definitions. Generally, a career is seen as an individual's journey through learning and work that brings out their intrinsic worth – their identity. It underscores the activities of a person that define their worth in terms of their achievements, work portfolio, and essence in life. A career is the work that you do as a profession that brings solutions and answers to a particular need or challenge in society. Career is more of service to others, other than you.

The Merriam-Webster dictionary explains a career as a profession that is undertaken as a permanent calling. The definition of a career mentions something eternal or permanent. Career, in essence, underscores the total summation of a person's profession in life, i.e., what an individual lives for and wishes to be identified with. It is not only about portfolios, positions, or companies you have worked for. It is about what you stand for, your passion, and the skill you have developed, which consolidates your worth. Your career is your life, so choose one that syncs with your intrinsic worth.

Career is what you live for and seek to be identified with! It is more altruistic rather than egoistic.

Things to Know about Career

1. Career is eternal; it is not temporal, it may evolve or change along the course of self-discovery and opportunities, but note that it is forever and given from above; hence, you will be accountable for it.

2. It is your calling, assignment, and profession in life – Without this, your existence is meaningless. Consider something you love and have a passion for.

3. A career is not the job you do, but the work you do. Work is different from your job. Your job may not be your career, but your work is your career. Job is what earns you an income, but your work is what earns you satisfaction and at the end of the day gets your needs met.

4. A career is not man-made or man-ordained – it is God-given and Man-driven. It is not about you but about God and humanity. Career is God and man at work to achieve His will. This is the reason you need God in the choice of a career path.

5. It must be needs-driven, solution-based, and altruistic. When ego and ambition cloud your mind and heart, it leads to a lot of undesirable endings and does not help you make the right career decision. Your choice of career must be for the benefit of society and

community and not just yourself.

Having made these points clear, it is essential to bear in mind that because our career represents our profession, we need to invest a great deal of time and diligence in understanding ourselves and conducting informed research through counselling, mentorship, and volunteering to inform our career decisions. Everybody has been endowed with thoughts, enthusiasm, abilities, and talents that make us unique and special. These virtues mostly come from within and can't be erased, even though they can be rendered redundant.

We can only enhance or sharpen them through mentorship and training programs. If we are to give attention to this subject – career, there will be lots of solutions and interventions in our world today. Unfortunately, the complexity of our world today in terms of policies, systems, and structures has made it difficult for people to pursue their passion and calling. Lately, people choose their careers based on money, power, fame, family prestige sometimes, influence, and image. Peer pressure influences people to enter into undesirable ventures. The only way to be truly satisfied is to do what you believe is a great work that reflects your intrinsic worth – something worth dying for or being remembered for.

Self-awareness and Career Alignment

'Before I formed you in the womb, I knew you, before you were born I set you apart and appointed you as a prophet unto the nation'. – Jeremiah 1:5

As mentioned earlier, the masses are in pain, regret, and confusion because of the wrong choices they made. One important aspect of life which needs no hasty decision is making a career decision as it literally constitutes the very essence of our life. Until we have full knowledge of who we are and that which God has made us to be, it will be difficult to understand exactly the career path or calling which will bring us fulfilment. What gives life meaning is our ability to be a solution to others' problems; we find fulfilment in helping or making others smile – this indeed should be the goal of pursuing any career. A career path that leads many into destruction and pain is never worth pursuing, no matter the material benefit it promises. What you have no knowledge of will eventually destroy you. Sir John Whitmore, a career coach in his book *Coaching for Performance* writes;

> *'I am able to control only that which I am aware of. That which I am unaware of controls me – Awareness empowers me.'*

Most part of our lives should be lived in self-discovery. The discovery of who we are will save us from a lot of trouble and unnecessary harm. No one can have an idea of who they are unless they know God. God created us; hence He will be the best person to inform us about our identity.

Kindly pause and think about the questions below. These are some keys to self discovery. Take your time and go through the questions below.

> *'Quality questions create a quality life. Successful people ask better questions, and as a result, they get better answers'* – *Tony Robbins.*

I.   *How do you describe yourself?*
The question of self-identity should not be taken lightly. This question gives you the opportunity to look within yourself and tell the whole world who you really are. Who you include your potential, passion, gifts, and talents. Use simple words to paint a picture of who you are – you are the only one who can tell everyone who you are. So who are you really?

II.   *Where am I, and why am I here?*
Like using a GPS which tells us at every point in time wherever we find ourselves, it is important to know your present location in life. This question has to do with your current state and stage in life. You must quiz yourself about how you got to where you are now. Self-discovery leads you to purpose – why am I here? Your potential, passion, gifts, etc., give you an idea of why you are here. After knowing who you are and identifying why you were born, it will become real to you whether you are in the right or the wrong career trajectory.

III.   *What activities or things give me the most joy and satisfaction?*
Please note that joy is not the same as happiness. There are certain activities that give momentary happiness but leave unending pain and regrets in your life. Joy is the continual swelling of gratitude from within that leaves one with peace and inner tranquility despite the happenings around. For example, saving a cat from drowning, winning a competition, etc.

IV.   *What are the first two words that describe me?*
These words basically represent or summarize what you stand for, i.e., your general identity. Take some time to think about these words.

V.   *How do others describe you?*

This part of the exercise makes you know what others think of you. It could be your friends, family, your teachers, or anyone who has a connection with you. Ask them to be honest about who they know you to be. From this, you can compare who you think you are and what they think of you and make a good conclusion about your identity.

SWOT Analysis

STRENGTH	WEAKNESSES	OPPORTUNITIES	THREATS
What are you very good at doing? (your own assessment and what others have consistently told you)	What are you not good at? This is an area where you get negative feedback from your own assessment as well as others' (which needs improvement).	What are the opportunities around you that you can take advantage of to help you achieve your goals?	What are the obstacles in your way which make it difficult to achieve your goals?
•**Internal and has to do with YOU.** •**Within your control** •**Current reality**	•This is internal and has to do with YOU. •Within your control •Current reality	•External and outside of yourself. •Outside your control •Current/future	•External and outside of yourself •Outside your control •Current/future.

VI.   *What is that one thing around me that I would love to change?*

The things happening around you that 'break' your heart. It is as if you are the only one who sees something wrong.

Something you can die for.

VII. *What activity would I love to do all my life, even if I will not be paid for it?*
Pursue what you love and monetize it, don't pursue money do things you believe is a great career that makes money pursue you.

VIII. *What is there to discover about yourself: what is your most surprising self-discovery?*
There are unique peculiarities within you, you may not have an idea about them, but it gets you to do things that surprise you when you do them. List these unique qualities down, they are there for a reason.

IX. *What have you discovered about yourself that you were not very aware of before?*
With the help of these questions, you will at least have a picture of who you are. Having gone through this whole complex, the next thing to do is to undertake a personality assessment. Certain career choices demand peculiar kinds of personality traits. Generally, all personality traits are grouped into two, but in some cases, three.

1. **Extroverts:** These are outgoing, socially confident, and people-oriented individuals—any time they find themselves at social events, they become the centre of attraction. They derive their importance or worth from acceptance and attention. This class of people thrives on talking to others, and they feel more creative when doing so. Some likely professions that match this personality trait include Law, Sales management, Event planning, Cosmetology, Public Relations, Music, Journalism, and also

the Arts and History discipline. These are the choleric and sanguine personalities.

2. **Introverts:** According to one modern school of thought, introverts tend to fall within one of four main categories: unsocial, thinking, anxious, and inhibited. These are the exact opposite of extroverts. An introverted person loves to spend time alone and with family. They feel exhausted and uncomfortable by a large crowd. They engage more of their mind and are good decision makers – examples of careers that may suit such personalities include Electrical or Electronic Engineer, Data Base Administrator, Aerospace Engineer, Interior Designer, Accountant, Statistician, Medical Doctor Etc.

3. **Omniverts/Ambiverts:** It is also seen that no person is completely extroverted or introverted. Everyone has a little trait of each of the above. Omniverts are people whose traits are determined by the kind of people or situations around them. They adjust as the occasion demands. Ambiverts are versatile people who can easily fit into their surroundings. In a low-intensity environment, an omnivert may act as an introvert but will be an extrovert in a stimulating environment. Teaching, Pastoring, Virtual Assisting, Public Relations, paralegal jobs, etc., are some examples of career choices for ambiverts.

*NB: You can obtain full explanations and detailed notes on these in the book, '**Self-Discovery**' by the same author.*

Choosing a Career That Reflects Your Intrinsic Worth

Now that we have attempted to help you have an idea of who you are, you can now make an informed decision on what you really want out of life –Career. Besides knowing who you are, it is important to know and understand your passion, talent, and your desire. This will help you to build capacity in terms of skill acquisition and training to sharpen them.

1. **Passion** refers to a strong and barely controllable emotion or feeling towards an idea, a person, or an object. Without passion or zeal, purpose cannot be accomplished. Passion is the 'mitochondrion' – the energy supply house that will help you to be consistent and persistent in achieving your career. Passion is not only inherent but can be built or revived. It must be directed into the right channel for the right course. Skills are also a requirement needed in the choice of a career.

2. **Talent and Skill** Talent basically denotes a person's ability coming from knowledge, practice, and aptitude, to do something well – competence. Skill is one of the basic requirements in choosing a career. When a person shows much passion and zeal with an accompanying skill in a particular area or profession, he or she could be mentored or trained to achieve a career in that area.

3. **Desire** is something you crave or need temporarily such that if it is not gotten, frustration sets in. Desire is an intense hunger of the soul for something to be satisfied or accomplished. Without a strong desire to get work done, it

will remain undone. You must have a strong desire for a career in order to have it accomplished. What is your desire in this life as far as your career is concerned? What have you done about it?

You will be able to know a person's career or calling by following these simple career theories. It is important to understand that rights, morality, truth, etc., are endowed by our Creator – so is our Career. You did not just happen to be on earth. Your reason for existence is an answer to a need somewhere in the world. In summary, you have been born to be a solution. No matter the circumstances concerning your birth, you need to understand that you have a purpose, a calling, and a mandate to accomplish.

This mandate can only be accomplished through your career. The neglect or ignorance of this mandate will not only affect you negatively but also affect many people of the nations of the world to whom you have been assigned. The choice of your career must evidently and primarily reveal your purpose on earth. Invariably, our career must lead us to fulfil the will of God for our lives.

Nothing was left to chance in God's plan for creation. He purposely planned our existence and purpose through a mapped-out intricate network. Your career is not about the religion you belong to, political affiliation, family, or even yourself; it is about God's eternal plan for mankind. When we understand this idea, we will be careful how we plan and execute our life choices. Detailed research conducted at different ages and career levels to ascertain how people got to know their career and the extent to which they have been satisfied in pursuing that path showed that about 85% of the workforce wake up on Monday morning with high blood pressure. The reason is the start of a stressful week. Many people are unhappy with the kind of work they find themselves doing. They wake up already stressed because of the work on the table. Consider these theories below:

- *Intrinsic Worth-Theory:*

It is the value or unique attribute a person has that is part of their genetic make-up. An individual's intrinsic worth is that intangible quality that gives him or her relevance other than what they possess. Intrinsic worth is that intangible quality that gives a person value other than what they have acquired materially. An individual's intrinsic worth is a natural phenomenon that gives them relevance. Most of the time, the individuals with such unique virtue may not be conscious of it, as it comes naturally through learning, their behaviours, actions, and general disposition. This personal worth is clearly seen and noticed by people with whom we have shared precious moments with. The quality of love, care, intelligence, unique voice, strength, etc. are examples of a person's intrinsic worth. Something you naturally do without any form of compulsion. Our intrinsic value is mostly linked to our passion, interest, likes, skills, and talents.

Our intrinsic worth also denotes valuable reflexes that are stored in our subconscious minds and part of our genetic make-up. There are certain default qualities and peculiar traits (talents, attributes, or interests) that every child in their developmental stage exhibits. These qualities are mostly identified by parents and people who socialize with them. Some mothers, during pregnancy or at the point of delivery, are able to tell what their unborn babies will become.

However, every child is unique and hence, must receive special attention to help nurture their talents and interests for them to materialize.

> *'Train up the child in the way he should go, and when he grows, he will not depart from it' – Prov. 22:6*

When we are able to give quality attention to the development and training of children, which is a principal responsibility of parents, it opens a platform that springs them unto success and in doing so, makes it difficult for them to fail. The passion, interest, and likes of an individual are developed when deliberate guidance and support are given. Each one of us had interesting childhood memories – memories filled with creativity and happiness. Kids engage in activities and talents which subtly reveal their interests and passion. This theory led to the introduction of Career Day in many schools. It is very important for children to be guided and mentored into fulfilling this desire and interest. Some people are born teachers, some excel in sports like football, and others are good in other fields – all of which can be traced to their childhood desires and aspirations. Get the Self-Discovery book for more information.

· *Temperament Theory:*

Choosing a programme of study and, consequently, a professional career is a challenging process that is influenced by several factors (external and internal). One of such is temperament. Temperament makes up an individual's personality. Besides the required professional competencies, one needs a thorough knowledge of their temperament.

Basically, we have several personality traits. Some of

these traits or dispositions may include cultural sympathy, social initiative, flexibility, open-mindedness, and emotional stability. All of these should be a major determinant when choosing a career. Understanding the type of personality you have is a major factor that will give you an idea of which career path will best suit you. I have explained this already under the personality assessment.

Choosing a career based on a person's temperament helps the individual have a satisfied life. There are four major temperamental traits; choleric, sanguine, melancholic, and phlegmatic. With the help of this theory, you will be able to know the career that will best fit the temperament you possess. Your temperament – social and biological make-up should be a guide to what you are comfortable with. You may sign up for our Career Direct services to help you understand the career path that will be of great benefit to you and society.

· *Divine Determinant*

This is the first and basic way of having an idea of what you have been ordained to do. One of the secrets in life is to know and understand that what we see has its footing in the unseen. What we see in the physical is just a figment of what is taking place in the spiritual. In order to have a successful life and career, you must be connected to a Supreme Being (God). Through dreams, visions, and spiritual encounters, you can know what exactly your career path is. This is indeed the first and most important career determinant in our lives. Anyone who says they do not need God is just like saying I do not need air to breathe; ultimately, you will end up dying within the next second. It is so evident that we need God in all of our lives. It is quite a major risk to make decisions in life without considering the giver of life.

In having a meaningful career path, it is instructive to spend a lot of time in God's presence through his word, prayers, and sometimes even through fasting, for him to lead us into what he has planned for us to be. When you joke with your spiritual life, you may end up making a wrong choice with your career. In prayer, ask God to reveal to you what he wants you to become. In prayer, we receive words of confirmation, affirmations, and divine illumination through our spirit. This, for me, is the surest way to know the career path for your life.

· *Sociocultural Orientation*

Our sociocultural orientation is another key determinant in choosing a career. Sociocultural orientation refers to those large-scale forces within culture and society that affect our thoughts, feeling, and behaviour. A society or a culture that believes that women should not work but become housewives will ultimately impact the career dimension of the girl child. The environment in which we grow goes a long way in determining our career choices. The environment and cultural fibre in which one finds him/herself has a great impact in determining an individual's career path. Join the Career Direct programme to know more about this.

Finally, having said all these, I will add that it is important to understand the world in which you find yourself. Consider your family, community, friends, and loved ones. Look at the inappropriate things around you which breaks your heart. Look for something you are happy and fulfilled doing or problems you feel satisfied solving and develop a career around it. Always remember your career must bring hope to humanity and ultimately bring glory to God. Get the **Self-Discovery** book now!

3|Developing a Career Plan

Developing a career plan can be a tough challenge. Many people would rather have others write it for them than do so themselves. It is important that you dedicate much attention and quality time to writing down what you believe is a great career plan for your life. Failure to develop a career plan in itself is a decision awaiting a possible career struggle. A career plan must be 'SMART' – Simple, Measurable, Attainable or Achievable, Real, and Timely. As noted earlier, you need to consider your capacity – passion, skill, and environment, as these will help you choose an attainable career. This is not to say one should settle for less; every career path is achievable so long as you have the passion and stay focused on it. The career you choose must be well-understood and measurable. When we say your career plan must be measurable, we mean it must bring a solution or lead one to fulfill the purpose for pursuing it. For example, if you choose a career to be a clean water ambassador because your passion is to eradicate water borne-diseases, this career path must lead you to fulfill such great ambition. At the end of the day, we must see polluted water bodies being refined.

Furthermore, your career plan should be attainable – it should not be something that frustrates you or is difficult to attain. One's inability to execute their calling may mean that in the first place, it was probably not their career, or possibly they did not build much capacity or seek counselling before taking that path. Lack of career counselling and mentorship could also account for the failure to realize a person's career choice. Unrealistic career plans cannot be achievable. It must be time-bound and of the essence. A delayed career accomplishment is as bad as not starting at all. When you put things in perspective, it will guide you into achieving them.

- *What is a Career Plan?*

A plan is a detailed proposal for doing or achieving something. A career plan serves a variety of purposes based on one's area of interest and specialty. A career plan refers to a multi-year outline of where you want to be or take your career or profession. Without clarity about where you are going, you cannot know what is required to get there. A career plan helps one identify and acquire the necessary skills, education, and experience needed to get to where a person desire to be. This information helps one choose the right courses and programmes at any educational level.

Most of us complete school with the hope that we will be employed, and hence fail to develop a career map or direction aimed at fulfilling our purpose on earth. It is very important to note that when you fail to develop a career plan for your life, it becomes difficult to have a smooth career transition. Every serious student and graduate must have a career plan. Every career plan consists of a short and a long-term course of action, such that the short one becomes a ground on which the long-term plan would be achieved.

The short-term career plan basically stresses on the development of realistic goals and objectives, that is, "What is my passion? What makes me different from others?

What do I really want to achieve in this life?" etc. In

developing a career plan, one must try as much as possible to remove all forms of distracters like peer and elderly pressure. They can give advice and guidance but should not coerce you into accepting what they believe is a great career decision. One needs to patiently look within one's self, slowly and reasonably, in order to obtain the right and best descriptive plan. The following nugget will help you plan your career.

- *Analyze your current and future lifestyle (Ideal lifestyle)*

How is your lifestyle now, and how do you ideally want your lifestyle to be in the near future? Is your current lifestyle, in a way leading you to achieve the future you want to live? Always remember that we look at our past as a bedrock on which we live in the present, and our present life is a precursor to our future life. The picture of the future we want to be featured in is hidden in our daily routines. The future does not create itself – it does not happen by chance. We create the future we want to see. Will what I am doing now help me achieve what I expect to see in my life tomorrow?

- *Analyse your likes and dislikes (Identity check)*

Who are you, really? Are you pretending to be someone you are not? Many of us are living lives of pretense and deception. We find our worth in the clothes we wear, the phones we use, and other material products, forgetting that these brands came into being through the hard work of other people who identified a need area in the society. Your worth is intrinsic and not extrinsic. It is that quality within you that cannot be bought but can be 'sold'. What we fail to recognise is that we deceive ourselves when our value is seen in what we possess; what if we lose them? What then becomes of you? Do you live your life because you want everyone to like you? Then it is better you start selling ice cream.

You need to love yourself, own yourself, and appreciate who you are; this is the starting point of making the right decisions. Be bold and proud of your identity. Create that boundary and respect, which would be difficult to break. Outline what you stand for and what you stand against by enlisting your likes and dislikes, thereby defining who you are. Knowing what you like and what you detest will help you choose a career that will not be contrary to your personality.

· *Analyse your passion (purpose of being)*
What gets your attention the most? What drives you and steals your attention until you have attained this desire or object? Pay attention to that inherent and subconscious interest and field that you love and are in love with, and start pursuing it because that is the reason for your being. This is very important and critical as it is the centre of what you are going to pursue. You need to answer the question- why am I here?

· *Take a look at your strengths and weaknesses*
No matter how beautiful, intelligent, and right one can be, we may have weaknesses that might be detrimental to our progress. Examples include procrastination, laziness, forgetfulness, etc. As you identify these, make conscious efforts to work on your weaknesses while taking note of your strengths. Knowing these will keep you updated about who you really are.

· *What is your definition of success?*
What do you call success? Is it when you are at the top of your

class, make a lot of money, etc.? Define your boundaries of success so that you don't become frustrated and unproductive.

· *What is your dream job?*

Your dream job is the job that brings you ultimate peace and satisfaction in life. List about five dream jobs and choose the first three. Forget about the last two and only focus on the first three.

· *Analyse your current situation*

At this juncture, take stock of your life. Are you satisfied with how you are living your life? Are you making headway as to achieving your future status? If no, then embrace change. It is now or never.

After carefully examining all these points, I believe you have a clue as to what you really want to achieve in life. What you should do next is plan your career. The following steps will be beneficial in making a comprehensive career plan.

1. What do you actually want to commit your life to (passion and purpose)?

2. Conduct detailed research and gather information about the career identified above from prospective consultancy services, mentorship, and career coaching summits. You can sign up for our career direct services at LUP Consult Limited.

3. Identify the qualifications and skills needed to walk the desired career path.

4. Compare your current qualification with that of the career

you want to achieve, and develop a plan to get qualified.

Typically, a career plan should be updated annually in anticipation of future developments. You have to find an effective way of measuring your progress. Below is a sample career plan.

SAMPLE CAREER PLAN

Career Goal:

To become an International Broadcast Journalist (Reporting new stories on an International News Network)

Requirements:
- Training in journalism or a degree equivalent
- Critical thinking and excellent communication skills
- Time management and service orientation
- Ability to monitor and assess situations.
- Good writing and reporting skills
- Ability to learn new strategies quickly.

Skills and Interests:
- Periodic contribution of short stories to Daily Graphic
- Volunteer newscaster on a campus radio station
- Serve on the editorial board as the editor of the high school magazine
- Scored grade B in both English and French literacy at the high school level.

Strategies to achieve the above:
- Get a degree in journalism: Ghana Institute of Journalism.
- Take up an appointment as a broadcaster at the Sompa FM newsroom.
- Obtain a Postgraduate degree in Mass Communication.

- Submit stories for local and international awards.
- File stories to International Media Networks.

51

The picture of the future we want to feature in is hidden in our daily routines.

4|Personal Branding

'Man look on the outward appearance, but God looks at the heart' – 1 Samuel 16: 7

The world today awaits the emergence of great minds, philosophers, and technocrats – men and women of great acumen, character, and integrity with great hunger and thirst for change. In this day and age, it is not enough to acquire certificates. The desireof communities, nations, and families is for people who are determined to bring unparalleled positive change. This change will only be realized through a determined and regenerated mindset rooted in a conscious effort of intentional living.

Men and women who have achieved great laurels and brought hope to their generation are not extraordinary in their looks or people with great stature. Some common trait we can see in this class of individuals is the desire for change, passion, sacrifice, and discipline. When we look at the Gates, the Buffets, and the Dangotes, we see a hunger and a desire backed with a passion for leaving a legacy, a legacy of hope for themselves and their generation. No matter how we may brand them as doing all these out of selfishness, we cannot deny the impact of their efforts all around the globe. Ken Blanchard, an astute educationist, once said in one of his speeches,

> *'My mission statement is to be a loving teacher and an example of the simple truth that helps me and others to awaken to the spirit and presence of God in the lives of others.'*

He goes on to talk about the fact that he mentions God because, often, we think that the biggest addiction in the world is our human ego where we start to think that we are the centre of the universe and forget that primarily, we are here to serve and give and not the other way round. He actually said –

> *"Do not do something for someone else with the desire to get something back, but rather be passionate about it because it's the right thing, but watch what will come back."*

The point worthy of note is that, for you to succeed in this life, you need a mindset born out of a mind-shift. You must have a mind not built or set on the usual standard of the world. You may seem ordinary now, but there is something more to your life that makes you extraordinary. You must learn to build a brand, an idea, or a system that helps you stand out and easily gets identified out of the crowd. Many people, mostly graduates, for want of a better life, settle for anything at all cost and end up wasted. This is because they have no idea about their intrinsic worth. Until we know who we are – our value and mandate in life, we will never be able to rise above ourselves.

Personal Branding Explained

Personal branding is a process of developing a 'mark' that is created around a person, business, or organisation's name and career. You use this mark to express and communicate your skills, personality, and values. Everyone can build a brand and cultivate their power to stand out and be unique despite the existing competition. Your brand is your core competence, your uniqueness, and your 'trademark.' It can be a way of service, taste, logo, etc. It will be difficult to make an impact without an active brand. Brands are not built overnight. It is a combination of hard work, perseverance, and consistency.

Your Brand Is Your Identity – Vision, Mission, and Values

When people say they want to build a personal brand, the first thing that comes into their minds is the number(s) – number of Instagram or Twitter followers. Building a personal brand goes beyond numbers. It means providing so much value and uniqueness that people begin to associate your name with the idea of what it means to be successful in that particular field. In building a personal brand, you must bear in mind that you are creating an identity that is associated with your life. The brand must therefore revolve around your mission in life – intrinsic worth (your assignment, calling, and reason for existence). Second, you must clearly outline what you hope to achieve in the near future (Vision). Finally, outline values and principles that will help you achieve the above. Your brand must follow the SMART and SWOT analysis – it must be unambiguous and reflect your life. Many people, by their actions, character, association, and attitude over the years or in their past, have messed up their brand. It is very important to note that whatever we do subtly affect our brand.

You are only going to be as good as the people you surround yourself with. So if you find yourself surrounded by people who constantly make you doubt yourself and make you question your self-esteem, and they do not support or make you feel loved or appreciated, then it's better to be alone.

Personal branding is about the association you keep. Personal branding also means when people market themselves and their careers as brands or create an asset by defining an individual body, clothes, etc. It is an ongoing process of establishing a prescribed (positive, daring, and challenging) image or impression in the mind of employers (the target) about one's self. I have summarized how to build an intrinsic brand that will make you become irresistible and daring into four acronyms – MAWP. This is illustrated below:

Employers always aim at making profit, expanding their businesses, and obtaining all the benefits attached to success. This mentality and mindset built by employers have made them critical and careful with the kind of employees or labour they employ. Organisations haunt not necessarily academically apt people; they look for a combination of intelligence and creativity in individuals. In chapter two of the *Building a Lasting Career Brand* book, I have shared a few thoughts on the values or elements that help graduates and employees from all walks of life to build character and capacity for life.

Mindset (Belief System)

This is the first and most important element in building a personal brand. Mindset is a composition of the personality and the belief system of an individual in decision-making or the general sphere of life.

The mindset of an individual is the engine room where the very life of the person is defined. A person with a negative or corrupted mindset can never produce anything beneficial.

> *As a man thinks in his heart (mind), so is he [what our mind is full of is what makes our mindset and, ultimately, our personality].*

Your mindset is your life-set, which is the true reflection of who you are. There is a slight and somehow confusing difference between the mind and the brain. Neuroscientists, philosophers, theologians, and psychologists have had an unending debate(s) about the link and difference between the mind and the brain. The fact I have gathered is that,

> *There is no mind without a working brain and no functioning brain without a mind.*

The brain is the physical organ made up of cells, blood vessels, and nerve pathways, i.e., the tangible and visible white ligament that is beneath the skull of the head. In summary, the brain can be touched and seen when opened. The mind underscores the unseen part of the brain, e.g., thoughts, emotions, dreams, and memory. One of the ways to have a great personality and unique branding is to build, train and develop one's mind, which will lead to an excellent mindset. In some books, the mind is used interchangeably with the soul. An individual's behaviour and actions can be traced to the state of their mind.

As a believer in the person and works of Jesus Christ, I have learned from the word of God to guard, train and restrain my mind from contaminations – evil thoughts and imaginations, so I will be pleasing to Him and humanity. The mindset is built through our senses. According to leading scientists, what we feed on has a great impact on our brain and affects the mind. A healthy mind lies in a healthy brain. What we see, touch, and listen to over the years has a subtle way of affecting our reasoning and how we respond to our environment. Our environment is one of the major determinants of our mindset. What we set our minds on becomes our mindset. What you feed your mind on is a brand you are building, which will be visible soon. A guy who sets his mind on watching pornography can never handle a woman with dignity – he sees her as a sex object rather than a person of value.

How to Develop a Great Mindset

There is something I have seen and noticed about human beings. One might disagree with me on this, but I have observed that the natural man's thoughts and imaginations are inclined to evil. There is a natural tendency to do evil than good, hence the need to train and develop a quality mindset. A great mindset is always possible; one needs a lot of determination and commitment to achieve this. Below are some suggested ways of building a great mindset:

• **Reckon that you need a great mindset**. You can only say this when you have accepted you have an unhealthy mindset by reason of the negative impact of your environment. Accepting your reality is the sure way to begin the change process of a quality mindset.

• **Seek help.** Get the help of a professional counsellor. Everyone needs a counsellor. At this stage, you need to open up to well-trained and trusted people, especially counsellors. I recommend a professional counsellor who is a Pastor. This is because the mindset is spiritual in nature, and the natural mind may not be able to comprehensively help get the desired result.

• **Decide to forget and delete negative experiences and associations.** In order to receive a great mindset, you need to be determined to let go and forgo associations, experiences, and environments that draw you into unhealthy reasoning.

• **Determine to develop and remember healthy and good attitudes and associations.** Endeavour through meditation and discipline to develop great experiences by associating with the right people, reading mind-engaging articles, a n d attending developmental programmes and activities that build a good and healthy mindset. You may engage in reading the Bible, informative magazines, and listening to thought-provoking songs and conferences. I recommend that you participate in the level-up Conference this year.

- **Get an accountability partner.** This individual will check up on you and put you on track. It should be someone who helps andencourages you to be a better version of yourself.

- **Finally, develop a healthy lifestyle.** It is said that a healthy mind lives in a healthy body. Have enough rest, stop worrying, andengage in stimulating thinking.

These are suggested steps that can aid in building a healthy mindset. Employers find candidates who are disciplined and morally sound, and with excellent acumen attractive, and will go to any length to recruit them into their Companies.

'Be ye transformed by the renewing of your mind that you may prove what good, acceptable and perfect will of God is' ROM 12:2B

Attitude

Attitude is not just everything; it is that one thing that makes a difference. A positive attitude is your most prized possession – one of your valuable assets. No matter your age, current position, gender, or marital status, a positive attitude can make an incredible difference in your life and in the lives of others. Your perception and outlook about the outcome of a situationlargely depend on your attitude.

It was Sundar Pichai the Indian American who told of a story about a group of guests who were invited to a function. During the snack break, as the waiters paced up and down to execute their duties, there was a scene created that almost marred the beauty of the function. A cockroach had fastened itself to the dress of one of the guests. When she became aware of the insect on her dress, she let out a scream, and to get the cockroach off her dress, she ended up spilling the drinks and all that had been served on the clothes of the other guests who sat close to her. The cockroach trying to escape from the unwelcoming guest got stuck unto the attire of another person causing a chaotic scene. Finally, it stuck itself on one of the waiters. The waiter after studying the insect for a while ambushed it, and gently picked the insect and sent it out, this act saved the day.

Our responses and actions to issues or challenges we find ourselves in are dependent on the kind of attitude we possess. We can complicate, reduce, or possibly stop the rippling effect of challenges that befall us when we learn to respond rather than react to issues around us. Problems or challenges are real and inevitable; they are part of our very existence. Until we come to terms with the reason things befall us, it will be difficult to know how to handle them. Most of the time, we ask the "Why me?" question, but the question should be, "Why not me?" When we embrace or take responsibilities for all our actions and inactions, we turn to respond to issues positively.

No matter how we may want to define it, building a positive attitude will help you stay focused. A positive attitude is one's trump card to success in this life.

The greatest discovery of the 21st century is rooted in the fact that people can always alter their attitudes by altering their mindsets. Everyone has the ability to improve the quality of every aspect of their life. However, they must first be willing to acquire the skills that will guide them to a place of self-identity. This will help them tap into the power of a positive attitude.

'You may not be able to change your height or body type, but you can change your attitude' – Keith Harrell.

Many graduates and employees have great ideas and knowledge but have bad attitudes. Many graduates fail when it comes to their attitude toward work and life. To a large extent, our mindset determines our attitude. Attitude is different from character. Character refers to the complex mental and ethical traits that distinguish a person from others. Attitude determines our character and also describes our brand.

Attitude is also the revealed state of the mind. It is a feeling or an emotion expressed towards a situation or an object. Our mindset influences our attitude, which in turn informs the kind of character we exhibit. In building a good career brand, we need a very optimistic and positive attitude toward everything we come across. We need a radical change in our attitude as individuals and as a nation. By so doing, we brand ourselves positively for success. One of the unhealthiest and most unproductive acts tearing our country apart is corruption, but another subtle element that is destroying and fuelling lots of activities bedeviling our country is our attitude – especially our attitude towards national development. Politicians, national leaders, and state officials who are dabbling in unlawful and immoral acts lack a good image of themselves. Corruption has a way of reducing creativity among professionals. Corruption puts personal interest over national interest. All these are born out of wrong attitudes.

During my undergraduate studies at the University of Cape Coast – (UCC), I used to look forward to the Public Administration lecture session – sorry to say, not because of the lecturer, but the course content. In summary, this course explains and enlightens the course reader about the matrix and intricacies surrounding the operations of the public and government sector job space. One of the points that kept me thinking was the fact that people who work in the public or government sector are called public servants; that is to say, these are people who have decided to serve the nation. I do not know anyone who would 'really' want to serve in Ghana because many people eschew the word service. In our day and age, only a few want to serve. So when I see people who get so excited, especially when they are appointed to work in the public space, or better put, for the government, I really commend them because it is not easy to serve.

Serving the nation in whatever capacity is a herculean task and must not be taken lightly at all. It is sad how people (especially politicians) hide behind the name 'public servants' and the phrase 'I stand for the nation's interest' to misuse money and sign budgets in their own parochial interest. We have redefined the purpose of service into commerce and an opportunity to become rich. The young graduate aspiring to become a politician is not doing so for service to mankind but for commerce. Our mindset and attitude are the reasons we are failing as Africans.

Another unhealthy attitude exhibited by public sector workers is indifference. This has to do with the 'I do not care spirit.' In our workplaces (especially in government offices), when a worker tries to do something that will bring hope and change to the organization and the nation at large, coworkers, especially those who have nothing better to offer, feels threatened by the good initiative and intention of these workers and try to find ways of backbiting and discouraging them, most of the time with the phrase, 'Is this your father's property? Are you the one to make the nation better?' These accusers go the extra mile to use their position to sabotage the good efforts of such attempts for innovation.

This defeatist attitude of ours has resulted in many deaths and unfortunate happening among these amazing talents who seek nothing but the best for the nation. As a nation, we need a mind shift for a great mindset that will build in us a great attitude for national development. Developing positive attitude value propositional labour force is very important and cut across transcultural barriers and are good for personal branding. As a graduate or an employee, there are certain attitudes one needs to unlearn, there are others to learn, and there are some to relearn.

Listed below are examples of some good attitudes for a great future. Before I enumerate them, you need to; Understand the power of attitude – it can make and unmake you, attitude may not be everything, but it does determine your success in life.

1. Choose to take control of your life. Whatever happens to you is not by chance, as many philosophers and realists would say, but it is by choice. What, where, and whoever we choose in life determines what we obtain in life.

2. Be determined to learn and develop a positive attitude, no matter the situation in which you find yourself. A person may choose to be the best version of themselves or remain as they are. Take charge of your life by choosing to be positive always.

3. Engage in a self-discovery exercise. This will help you know which attitude to let go of and the ones to propel you forward. Refrainfrom a bad attitude.

4. Find your purpose and passion and pursue it. Discover

5. What motivates you and build supportive relationships and associations around it. Determine to leave a legacy of a good brand – a positive attitude.

Attitude to Possess

1. Never stop trying. Develop an optimistic mindset. Always remember winners never quit.

2. Never underestimate your opponent. Your opponent is any other person other than yourself. Do not take such people for granted, be prepared to present a good defense and testimony anytime you meet one.

3. Cherish your talent. Give attention to your gift and

talent. Talents and gifts are divine and natural providence that subtly serves as a cardinal point to what you were born to do in this life. It will open many doors for you. I call them 'intrinsic capital'.

4. Learn to listen and be open-minded. Our generation lacks the culture to sit to listen. We are always on the go; we always want everything quickly and immediately. Developing the art of listening is the key to unending success.

5. Talk less, do more. In all circumstances, learn to do more. It is better to do more and talk less than talk more and do little. This comes with the quality of learning to be teachable and hardworking.

6. You always need to have an attitude. This attitude must be a positive one, of course. People with positive attitudes build the best personal brands. Best Wishes.

Learn the attitude of the Lion, Ant, Snake, Eagle, and Lamb – these will help you in your life's endeavour.

Words

'A good man's speech reveals the rich treasure within him, an evil-hearted man is filled with venom and his speech reveals it.' (Matthew 12:35)

Words are products of good or bad treasures within, and they come out the way they are communicated. One of the most important aspects of one's life is the ability to (communicate), and use words meaningfully. Your words define your life; words define your value and your personality. You are no better than your words. We can distinguish between a foolish man and a wise man by their words. The character of your words is the character of your personality. Your words are the expression, the manifestation, and the reflection of your life. It does not take long to know who a person is; all you have to do is to listen to them speak for a few minutes. This is because your words locate you.

In order to build or have a quality and outstanding brand, you must know how to speak, when to speak, where to speak, what to say, and to whom, this is called the art of communicating. Take a moment and think about how others describe you by the words you speak. Bad communication is one of the reasons many people will never have access to places of relevance and influence. Friends, it does matter how you speak and how you express yourself! You will always get better results if you speak nicely to others (even when you disagree with their opinion). Words are not just a mere collection of alphabets, words are spirit, and they give life or death to their hearers. Encouragement, motivation, and promotion – They all come through words. Likewise, discouragement, demotivation, and demotion come through words. Our words describe our personalities. We are in a dispensation where we joke with words. We use words loosely without thinking of or considering the impact they might have on others. Remember that Laws and decrees that can affect even generations yet unborn are enacted through words. Words are seeds we plant in our lives and others. They are a reflection of what is in our hearts or on our minds. In our schools, we are taught only how to formulate, construct and put words together to form sentences. Unfortunately, we are not thought the art of communication. Knowing this will at least put a check on our lines of discourse and the words we use in communication. I sit and imagine how well-educated men and women use vulgar, profane, and demeaning words to destroy the personality of their fellows, especially in times of challenges. Words of wisdom and knowledge come from a healthy mindset.

Say What You Mean and Mean What You Say! – Integrity in Communication

In our generation today telling a lie has become a culture and we see nothing wrong with it. Knowing how to trick, deceive and manipulate people with words (linguistic trickery) is now called being smart. The cost one pays for telling a simple lie far outweighs that which is paid for speaking the truth today. We need to learn to speak the truth always and speak positively about everything and ourselves, because we will be judged by our words. Be positive and optimistic in your communication. We are bounded by our words; people take you seriously when you walk the talk. Have you noticed that anytime one is being arrested, they are cautioned to remain silent or whatever they say could be used against them in the court of law? We may have the right to speak, but we will be held accountable by our words. Friends started losing confidence and trust in me because at a point in my life I used words loosely, in trying to please everyone, I would say one thing and do another. It is very important to mean what you say and say what you mean- this quality builds trust. When we do not act on our words, we break ourselves and lose the trust of people. One of the ways to strategically position oneself in the mind of prospective employers is being a person of integrity in your communication. What you write on your CV or resume should be the exact picture of who you are. Many people (graduates) do not resemble what they have assembled. When you develop the skill and conscious effort to be a positive communicator by looking at the good side of issues, it grants you leverages wherever you go. Learning to confess positive things and speaking the truth is one of the ways of building a good personal brand. Think about it. Create your world of difference by speaking positively.

Your Word is Your Brand

Building a lasting brand has to do with the kind of words that stem out of your mouth – communication skill and style.

1. Engage yourself in the constant reading of sound materials. Continuously and habitually train yourself to read good and sound literature with stories and illustrations filled with soul-lifting ideas. Concentrate especially on those filled with words of wisdom, encouragement, and motivation.

2. Listen to sound music and conference videos, audio tapes, podcasts, and attend capacity-building conferences or seminars. Unfortunately, the content and context of our contemporary music make it difficult to have sound and understandable communication. Desist from content that seeks to promote alcohol, hatred, immorality, etc.

3. Learn to listen more rather than speak. You must know when to keep quiet and when to speak. The more you listen, the more you know.

4. Surround and engage yourself with people of sound and

wise communication. Avoid proud, noisy, and unrestrained communicators. Be conscious and mindful of what you say, how you say it, where it is said, and to whom you say it. It is called the wisdom of speaking.

5. Finally, learn to be assertive. Most people say unimaginable things when they are under pressure or in an uncomfortable situation (when they are hurt, in pain, or disappointed). Being able to express positive and negative ideas and feelings in an open, honest, and direct way helps create a congener atmosphere for healthy living. Being assertive helps one to recognise their rights whilst respecting the rights of others. Assertiveness allows people to take responsibility for themselves and their actions without judging or blaming others.

Personality (Stature)

Personality refers to the complex characteristics that distinguish an individual. It also denotes the totality of an individual's behavioural and emotional characteristics. It's the combination of both the internal and external predisposition of a person. It encompasses our emotions, thoughts, behaviours, moods, attitudes, and opinions. I define personality as a person's attribute in reality. There are two sides to an individual's personality – the internal and external. The internal determines the external. We are able to determine an individual's personality through their interactions with their environment. What I have explained so far deals with the internal attributes that make a part of an individual's personality. This section concentrates on a person's outward appearance and stature.

Every moment you live, you are being judged. People judge you within 60 seconds of meeting you. We are visual beings. On a first impression, 55% of who you are is judged by how you look – your visual, 38% by how you sound – vocal, and 7% by what you say- content. Learn the art of dressing i.e., dress according to your body shape or stature, dress for that particular assignment. Dressing sharp and grooming yourself well is not vanity; it is sanity. Dressing meaningfully and attractively is your trump card to unending success. Here are some tips for you.

1. **Colour Combination** – Be careful with the colour of your outfit. Find out the dress code before attending an important function. Your dress code attracts and repels in equal measure. Smartness has nothing to do with neither formal or casual dressing but being comfortable in your skin. Learn to know which colour looks good on you and best fits the occasion.

2. **A healthy body always looks good in a sharp dress –** In as much as the emphasis is placed on the type of dress, it is important to note that a neat and healthy body wills definitely look good in a smart dress. Take good care of your stature and health.

3. **Dress decently, be moderate, and yet sharp in your dressing** – Always dress for your assignment and what you believe is a great profession. Remember that your dress code is part of your brand. It is said that you will be addressed the way you are dressed.

An employer shared with me an encounter he had

with a very brilliant but unkempt prospective employee who came seeking an opening. He said, "This guy's CV was great and looked good but, unfortunately, when I invited him for further discussion, I noticed he had a bad breath and, sorry to say, 'strong presence' which actually put me off despite the great learning."

First impression lasts long and says a lot about us. 'Man always looks at the outward appearance'. Customers always consider the brand and packaging of a product before its content. My dad shared an interesting story with me. He said someone stole a golden watch, and on reaching a bus station, he noticed some police officials were tracking him; even though he knew very well, they did not have the slightest idea of how he looked. The officials perceived the person was among the passengers on the last bus, so they had to investigate – upon entering the bus, they noticed this rascal and shabbily dressed guy who was sitting unconcerned at the corner of the bus. There and then, he was apprehended, handcuffed, and sent out of the bus. Seated at the extreme opposite of this innocent guy was the culprit – he was neat and executive in his appearance.

The moral of the story is that you dress the way you want to be addressed. Many young graduates lack this act. What you wear for an interview or any function, be it a dress or perfume you put on, tells a lot about your personality. In building a lasting brand, you must consider a healthy and morally sound appearance. That is not to say wear only expensive designer outfit; rather, I am saying wear something presentable, neat, and decent that suits the occasion. I believe this chapter, even though short, has been an eye-opener.

A great personality is one of the greatest assets any potential employee should not joke with because first impressions, as far as dressing is concerned, last long in the minds of prospective employers. It should be a lifestyle because nobody knows when an opportunity may come to you. Kindly note; in the workplace or wherever you find yourself, you need to be progressively responsible for everything that happens around you. There is no dignity in being a social misfit – it pays to be honest, humble, and truthful in all you do. Personal branding is what will give you credibility and celebration all your life. You can join the personal branding training class. See you at the top. Get more details on my award-winning book, *My Brand MyIdentity.*

5| Strategic Positioning – Self-Packaging

CVs/Resumes and Cover Letters

Now that we have clearly discussed the need for self-discovery that will help one achieve better personal branding, it is imperative we understand the dynamics in strategically positioning one's brand in the job market and also in the mind of prospective employers. Having a clearly spelled out and organized vision, qualifications, and abilities or experiences that match a job's demand is one of the ways to obtain an upper hand over colleagues who may be equally qualified. You can achieve this by developing good interview skills and having a neatly organized resume or curriculum vitae, popularly known as a CV, and a cover letter. That is what this chapter seeks to address.

Let's take a little time to judge this example. You had to choose between two tins of tomato paste, A and B. Tomato Paste A has a clearly labelled package indicating the manufacturing date, expiry date, nutritional content, and other relevant information, and Tomato Paste B, on the other hand, has none of the description and details of A. As a prospective customer who wishes to make a delicious and healthy meal for your restaurant, which one will you choose? No doubt most people will choose the Tomato Paste A over B. This analogy above spells out the importance and relevance of self-packaging – Strategic Positioning.

As a graduate, you must understand that in the 21st century, employers are keen on the kind of employees they recruit. This has caused many HR personnel to make the selection processes very competitive. In most cases, the process becomes so rigid that identifying the right and qualified candidate becomes difficult. As a result of not understanding the idea of the packaging, many good candidates fail to cross the first hurdle and never get close enough for the selectors to even know their worth.

When it comes to job search, self-packaging entails a lot; hence one must be adequately prepared. Curriculum vitae (CV), application letter (Cover letter), capability statement, design portfolio, publications, etc., are some of the tools and documents that can best help you to be well-positioned in your job search. Not all jobs may require all of these documents, but it is good to learn to write them. No other document is as important and persuasive as the curriculum vitae since it's your lawyer in the court of job selection and placement. A well-outlined and designed CV will indeed earn you the best place in your desired career. A poorly packaged CV and application letter will definitely find their way into the trash. Kindly take to heart some of these nuggets when drafting your CV and cover letters. It is always advisable to seek the consent of a career specialist or an HR personnel in order to have an outstanding CV. Sign up for our career-ready services at LUPCONSULT Limited. We have experienced experts who are able to review, design and help you produce a job-ready CV and Cover letter.

1. Curriculum Vitae (CV)/Resume:

Curriculum vitae is a Latin expression that is translated as the course of a person's life in a career. It is a written overview of a person's work life (academic formation, work experiences, publications, qualifications, etc.). A CV often aims to be a complete record of someone's career and ambition. It is, however, important to note that the curriculum vitae is an extension of a person's resume, which is typically a brief 1–2 page summary of qualifications and work experience. Many people say curriculum vitae and resume are the same, but ideally, if you consider the length, the purpose, and the layout of a CV and resume, you notice a slight difference. A resume spells out the summary of a person's skills and experiences over one or two pages – this can also be your profile related to a job. A CV is more detailed and lengthier. In general terms, they may serve the same purpose. Here are a few tips for packaging a winning Curriculum Vitae/Resume.

2. Attractive Page Layout and Structure

A neatly outlined layout and structured CV are easy to read and understand. Use appropriate font style, size, and line spacing to clearly map out the content and structure of your resume. A CV layout refers to the way in which the part or section of the CV is arranged or organized. The structure of a CV looks at how information is arranged according to the career plan. This is one of the critical parts recruiters look at. A poorly outlined CV will end up in the trash can- always remember that first impression lasts longer.

3. Solid and Relevant Content

When drafting the CV, the applicant must learn to be brief and express solid content. This is done by presenting and relating relevant information that has a great bearing on the position being applied for. You need to have adequate information about the job you are applying for so as to know what skill, experience, and qualification to highlight on your CV. Be concise and straightforward.

4. Adapt Your CV to Different Job

One of the cardinal mistakes most graduates or people in search of job opportunities commit is applying for different jobs with the same CV. The same resume cannot be used for different job portfolios or work. CVs must be drawn with the job or position being applied for in mind.

5. Work Experience

A summary of relevant and related work experience is very important to earn you a job placement. If there is no history of such, then maximum steps should be taken to get an experience on a job. People who do not have job experience must dwell on their skills and abilities as a major testimony of their ability to execute a job description. That is why internships and volunteering are important. You may sign up for our **internship** and **mentorship**services.

Non-academic Development Programs (extracurricular Activities)

Spell out non-academic and developmental activities which are connected to the job portfolio and the progress of the company at large. This will give a good impression of your versatility outside the work environment.

Specialized Skills and Abilities

This is one of the points you can dwell on as an advantage over your colleagues. Job seekers must be honest and truthful about their skills, abilities, and specialties. This aspect of the CV is very important as it reveals your value and your worth. These personal traits must be relevant, unambiguous, and useful to the development of the company. Relevant information concerning one's skills and specialty will be an advantage and a stepping stone to your dream Job.

- Summary or unique selling proposition
- Suitable length: Creating the right balance
- Regular updates

CVs must be regularly updated. That means the applicant seeking job placement must undertake relevant courses and attendtraining programs to enhance themselves. This will create a good picture of one's self.

This will be explained during the **Mentorship and Career Development Summit,** which is organised annually to equip and inform graduates and students on how to attack and succeed in their world of careers. Be on the lookout for such meetings. I have enclosed in this chapter some samples of curriculum vitae which will serve as a template to give you an idea of how to draft a CV. You could also search online for varied forms of CV layouts and structures.

SAMPLE OF RESUMES/CVS

❖ *CV of a Human Resource Professional*

Sarponmaa Safoa
P. O. Box AN000, Accra-North, Ghana
Phone: 111-111-111 E-mail: linda@mensah.com

Human Resource Development Professional

SUMMARY OF QUALIFICATIONS

Certified Human Resource Development Professional with 8 years of experience as a career specialist. Specialize in a range of services including career counseling, coaching, and job placement. Develop individual employment plans, goal-setting strategies, and networking skills. Demonstrated successful employment placement rate. Proficient in Microsoft Office programs and the use of database programs.

WORK EXPERIENCE

February 2010 – Present
SCF – BEACONS, ACCRA- GHANA Career Placement & Investment Specialist

- Provide career management services with a focus on helping customers secure employment.
- Conduct interviews, eligibility verification, career coaching, job search assistance, orientation, and regular follow-up on clients' individual employment plans.

January 2007 – February 2010
SCF-BEACONS, ACCRA-GHANA Career Development Support
Associate

- Led a group of five researchers working for a team of HR consultants and specialists.
- Provided training opportunities for students to enhance their educational skills and identify opportunities for program improvement and advancement.

February 2002 – November 2006
HUMAN CAPITAL SERVICES, ACCRA-GHANA Administrative
and Career Development Assistant

- Handled client inquiries and recorded information about the status of their requests and satisfaction levels.
- Entered and maintained all documents and case files in the database system.
- Provided services to customers and counseled students in tertiary institutions on career choices.

EDUCATION
- BSc. Business Administration (Human Resource Option) University of Ghana- Legon (1996-2000)
- Diploma in Human Resource Management Institute of Professional Studies, Manchester (Distance learning) June 2002
- Client Contact and Frontline Communication Skills 3-day course at Level Up Institute, Accra-Ghana (June 2004)

- Coaching for Career Success A week-long course at Level Up Institute, Accra-Ghana (November 2008)

ASSOCIATION MEMBERSHIPS

- Institute of Public Relations
- National Association of HR Professionals (NAHRP)

REFEREES

i.   Mr. Tom Smith General Manager Human Capital Services Accra. Telephone: (029) 111 111

ii. Ms. Angela Constance HR Manager SCF, Beacons Accra. Telephone: (024) 9995555

❖ *CV for a Fresh University Graduate*

PERSONAL DETAILS

Name	*Ebenezer Denson K.*
Address	*PMB 43, Kanda-Accra*
Email:	*k. smith@kanda.com*
Tel:	*(024) 000 000*
Date of birth:	*7th May 1986*

CAREER OBJECTIVE

I am a finance professional with a special interest in information technology, leadership development, and sports. I aspire to contribute my knowledge and skills in analysis and investment in a progressive corporate environment in which skills are relevant and appreciated.

PERSONAL SKILLS AND ABILITIES

- Proven leadership skills and ability to motivate
- Organisational and planning skills
- Strong writing and communication skills
- Ability to work independently or as part of a team
- Computer literacy.

EDUCATION

Bachelor of Commerce & Accounting, University of Cape Coast (2005-2009) Relevant Courses:

- Public Sector Economics
- Information and Markets
- Applied Policy Analysis
- Monetary Economics

- Micro Economic Theory
- Statistics for Business
- Microeconomics
- Monetary & Finance
- Introduction to Public Economics

ACHIEVEMENTS/RESPONSIBILITIES

- Treasurer, Business Students' Association
- Vice Chancellor's Excellence Awards Scholarship
- Hall President, Dynamic Hall (2008)

INTERNSHIP & VACATION WORK EXPERIENCE

July 2007 – Sept 2007: LUP Consult, Accra – Office Clerk

- Assisted with inventory control
- Handled telephone enquiries
- Filed customer accounts
- General administrative work

July 2008 – Sept 2008: Joy FM, Accra – Accounts Assistant

- Provided support for the accounting department
- Assisted with data entry and collating payment vouchers

Dec 2009 – Feb 2010: Volunteer, Springboard 2010 Road Show, legacy & legacy

INTERESTS

- Reading and going to the theatre
- Actively involved in hockey, soccer, and tennis
- Captain and coach of cricket teams
- Member of the Rotary Club of Accra West

SKILLS

- Proficient in online research
- Microsoft Office products (Access, Excel, PowerPoint)
- Desktop Publishing packages (Microsoft Publisher)
- Website design using Dreamweaver and Optiweb
- High level of keyboard proficiency and data entry experience

REFEREES

- Ms. Bernice Atikpoe Senior Lecturer Faculty of Commerce, University of Cape Coast (UCC) Tel: (042) 00000
- Mr. Abraham Michelles Manager Scf, Beacons International, Accra Tel: (024) 9999 555

NB: There are many who make the mistake of putting bulletins inthe referees section; this is not right. All the points must be in alignment.

Cover/ Application Letter

Another important document that accompanies the resume or CV is the cover letter, popularly known as the application letter. This isactually a contractual claim of one to prospective employers that declares an applicant's intention of interest to be an employee in that identified company.

❖ *Cover Letter Format*

The format below lists the information you need to include in the cover letter you submit along with your resume. The following guidelines will help in drafting a winning cover letter.

Take a look at the details below. This will give you an idea of what to write specifically in the letter.

A.   Your Contact Information
Name...
Address, City......................................
Phone Number...................................
Email Address....................................
Date...

B.   Employer Contact Information
Name...
Title...
Company..
Address, City......................................

SALUTATION

Dear Mr. / Ms. Last Name (If available),

BODY OF COVER LETTER

The body of the cover letter informs the employer what position you are applying for, why the employer should select you for an interview, and how you will follow up. This is the main letter – you need to be brief, confident, and professional to convince your employer. This must tally with what you have on your CV.

FIRST PARAGRAPH

The first paragraph of your letter should include information on why you are writing. Mention the position you are applying for and where you found the job listing.

MIDDLE PARAGRAPH(S)

The next section of your cover letter should describe what you have to offer the employer. This is where you must indicate your unique selling proposition (USP). Mention specifically how your qualifications match the job you are applying for. Remember, you are interpreting your resume, not repeating it.

FINAL PARAGRAPH

Conclude your cover letter by thanking the employer for considering you for the position. Indicate your availability for an interview or how you will follow up.

Respectfully yours,
Handwritten Signature (mailed letter)
Typed Signature
Name

How to Go About
Writing a SampleCover Letter

✓ *Address the Hiring Manager*

This is very important when it comes to writing a cover letter. Take your time to research to find out exactly who will be receiving your application. Always address the hiring Manager by their last name. This way, you can avoid the generic Dear Sir/Madam salutation and just address them by their name. It will also show the hiring manager that you are really interested in the position because you took the initiative.

✓ *Tailor the Cover Letter to Your Industry*

Many people make the mistake of using one or a general cover letter to apply for several jobs. By this, I mean to say that for everyjob, you will need a newly drafted cover letter tailored to suit the industry in which you are seeking to be employed. Every industryhas a format or style in which correspondence is written and processed. A cover letter for NGO jobs will be different from that ofa finance Job in a bank.

✓ *Show Value to the Company*

You need to express and show in simple terms how valuable you will be to the company once enlisted onto the team and equally prove how they stand the chance of losing a credible candidate if they let you go. Put ambition in check so you do not end up telling lies. Do not only focus on what the company can do for you but instead show what you will bring to the table and how It will benefit them.

✓ Be passionate!

When writing a cover letter for any job position, it is important you show the company how passionate you are about the position and the organisation as a whole. Talk about the vision and mission of the company, its products, and how you cannot wait to be on board to share in the activities and heights being attained, etc.

SAMPLE OF COVER LETTERS:
For Web Content Specialist

ELIZABETH E. AMEWONU

Web Content Specialist   Tel: 024 9999 555
nana.ama@yahoo.com
P.O. Box AN6816 Accra-North, Ghana

Mr. Emmanuel Mensah   *22nd February, 2010*
Managing Director, Clean Earth Aspirations,

+233-786-6829
hello@solutions.com
Accra, Ghana

JOB REFERENCE: WEB CONTENT SPECIALIST

Dear Mr. Mensah,

I am writing to express my interest in the position of web content specialist listed in the Daily Graphic of 15th February, 2010 and on businessghana.com.

I have four years of experience in building large consumer-focused websites. I have a track record of designing award-winning sites, with two of my concepts having won the coveted 'Website of the Year award' consecutively in 2007 and 2008. While much of my experiences have been in the business world, I understand the social value of the non-profit sector, and my business experience will be an asset to your organisation.

My responsibilities over the years have included the development and management of the site's editorial voice and style, the editorial calendar, and the daily content programming and production of the website. I have worked closely with the sales and marketing team to help them provide the most accurate information to their consumer audience. In addition, I have collaborated with the editors to present corporate content in a user-friendly, readily comprehensible text.

Experience has taught me how to build strong relationships with all departments at an organisation. I have the ability to work within as well as across teams. I can work with web engineers to resolve technical issues and implement technical enhancements, work with the development department to implement design and functional enhancements, monitor site statistics, and conduct search engine optimization. I look forward to the opportunity for an interview to discuss the prospects of my employment in greater detail.

Thank you for your consideration.
Sincerely,

Elizabeth E. Amewonu

SAMPLE OF COVER LETTERS:
For Web Content Specialist

ELIZABETH E. AMEWONU

Web Content Specialist

Mr. Emmanuel Mensah
Managing Director, Clean Earth Aspirations,

22nd February, 2010

+233-786-6829
hello@solutions.com
Accra, Ghana

JOB REFERENCE: WEB CONTENT SPECIALIST

Dear Mr. Mensah,

Independent schools such as Ridge Primary School require hardworking, organised, administrative staff to ensure that the school runs successfully and efficiently. My experience in administration and organizational skills would help contribute to the advancement of Ridge Primary School.

I have extensive administrative experience in an academic setting. For the past two years, I have worked at the early childhood centre at XYZ College, where I alternated between running activities for the children and answering phone calls, scheduling parent-teacher meetings, and performing Organizational tasks. I also served as an intern for the Principal at 123 Elementary School, undertaking a variety of office assignments while observing firsthandthe day-to-day duties of an academic administrator.

I have attached my resume and would be grateful if an opportunity for an interview is granted, so I could voice out how I could make a significant contribution to Ridge Primary School'sdaily operations. Thank you for your time and consideration.

After having all your documents well-arranged and organised, make sure you send them to two or more people – one with linguistic excellence and the other with a professional outlook to read through before you submit them. It is always advisable that after submitting an application online via email or whatever means required by the organisation, you submit a hard copy in person unless it is specifically indicated that applications should be submitted strictly online.

Thank you for your consideration.
Sincerely,
Elizabeth E. Amewonu

Tel: 024 9999 555
nana.ama@yahoo.com
P.O. Box AN6816 Accra-North, Ghana

6|Financing Your Career

One of the stumbling blocks to achieving a career goal is the lack of financial support or finance. Money sits as the topmost challenge on the list of difficulties many people, especially graduates, face in their quest to fulfil their career goals. This can be frustrating and heartbreaking. Many visions and ideas have not seen the light of day due to the lack of finances. I believe that despite this glaring reality, one should not throw in the towel, there is a way out. There are honourable ways of making money – it may take time, but surely it will become a mighty fortune. Do not wait to prepare, but prepare to 'wait', which means you should plan in advance.

Overcoming Financial Barriers to Fulfilling Your Career, the Cause

This chapter focuses on ways to prepare adequately to finance your dream career and further expand your financial frontiers, and attract income from different sources. Failure to understand the wisdom in this will make it difficult to navigate your way through life as far as your career is concerned. Whether you are a student or worker – whoever you may be, it is important to know that money rules the world today. It seems almost impossible to achieve anything great in life without money. Having one stream of income makes it a big deal to have a sound life.

'A feast is made for laughter, and wine makes merry: but money answers all things.' – Ecclesiastes 10:19

There is no problem in creating extra avenues for financial wealth so long as the means are legal and honourable. In this chapter, I will elaborate on how to tap into your inner strength and energy (unique qualities, skills, and talent) and transform it into financial wealth. This idea is premised on the model of multiple streams of income.

Wealth creation is a mentality rather than just a state of being. One can therefore create wealth by making important choices that will increase one's revenue. The primary mindset of everyone who desires to establish a great life for themselves should be to focus on how to multiply their income or diversify their sources of finance. Establishing multiple streams of income can be very tough and sometimes may seem almost impossible, but it has never been more than important in the world today. One major idea that has caused a lot of people – especially Africans not to think outside the box as far as financial independence is concerned is the high dependency ratio and our over-reliance on the government which most of the time takes forever to materialize. Until one takes responsibility for their life and well-being, it will be difficult to break free from poverty. The level of over-dependence – where the majority of the populace or family relations depends on just one individual or the government for livelihood and survival is the bane that has handcuffed Africa over the years from becoming the Star we anticipate.

Our culture, structure, and value systems have not

created a society where people own and take responsibility for their lives. This system has invariably not helped the young growing adult to think creatively because there is the mentality that 'an uncle' will provide. These people are not ATMs (Automated Teller Machines) which must automatically produce money when the need arises – they may get weary along the line, and if they fail, it automatically means their dependents have failed. I am not saying it is wrong to call on them when the need arises, but when someone entirely becomes your place of financial rescue, it prevents you from also tapping into your creativity and abilities, which is your number one money-generating tool.

Financing your Career

Now that you have a clear understanding of the career path and the kind of branding needed to complement it, you need to draw up a financial plan for achieving such a project. No Career laurel or path is too ambitious to achieve; once it is conceivable in mind, it is realizable. Consider the following strategies;

1. **Do not start late; start now!** Start with personal savings, get yourself a piggy bank (susu box), and a Career Investment Account – CIA as early as primary school. Parents must be intentional in their spending lifestyle and must set aside a portion of their earnings purposely for funding their wards career aspirations. The student also, as a way of complementing the efforts of parents and also as a personal goal, must set aside a portion of their monies for this same purpose. This act could be a great motivation to others who stand as potential sponsors to your future career. You need to own your life in the right direction. Sadly, I see lots of young children saving so much only to spend it at holiday parties, all in the name of entertainment.

**2.	Start small; begin with what you have.** Little drops of water indeed make a mighty ocean. Not all tips, coins, and 'dashes' given to us by friends and family are for now; they are for the future, so you need to learn to discipline yourself financially. My Pastor once said for every money earned or given; there is the seed part and the fruit part – eat the fruit and save or invest the seed.

**3.	Learn to be financially discipline.** As young people, so many things compete for our attention. The desire to become rich, to have the latest phone, sneakers, etc. I see so many young people using expensive phones and gadgets which could at least buy a piece of land or start a whole business. Learn to differentiate between your needs and wants

**4.	Frugality.** To be frugal means to spend wisely or calculatedly, taking thoughts of the future. We need to always spend with the future in view. Money has wings; today, it is here; tomorrow, it is gone, so you learn the wisdom of spending wisely.

**5.	Learn a money-generating trade or skill.** Take advantage of the internet to learn a trade or a new skill and develop a business around it. Do not wait till you are old enough. Business starts now. Samke Mhlongo-Ngwenya, Founder and CEO of TNC Wealth Partners says it is important to diversify your sources of income to ensure that you and your loved ones are financially secure.

'The current Ghanaian indebtedness level shows that people's income is not sufficient to fund their living and their aspirations and as a result, many resort to using debt. It is estimated that only 23% of Ghanaians have money left over at the end of the month. Therefore, we can assume that up to

77% of Ghanaians will borrow money to fund their needs,' she said.

She added that there are two broad categories of income streams – Active income stream and Passive income stream. Active income streams are those income streams that require activity to be generated. In the absence of the required activity, the income will not flow. Examples include board memberships, network marketing opportunities, and freelance work.

Passive income streams are those income streams where the income flow is not dependent on the activity of the recipient because the investment generates the income. Examples include rental income, dividend yield, and interest on a savings product.

Practical Ways of Financing Your Career

Freelance or Consulting

The simplest way to establish additional income is to sell your skill set to a wider audience through consulting or freelance work. This should be done in consultation with your current management and with their approval. This applies to people who are actively working and possess a sort after skills and abilities. One can be involved in consultation business and other freelance work that is connected to your job folio; this should be done in consultation with management to prevent anything like conflict of interest.

1. Join a Board of a Company

Board membership comes with personal liability, so an individual should ensure that they are comfortable with the corporate governance in the company they are joining and that they have the requisite competence to successfully execute their fiduciary duty as a board member. There may be allowances and bonuses for your decision and sitting.

2. Learn how to Trade Forex

It's advisable to open dummy forex accounts to test your aptitude for forex trading. If you have a knack for it, you could stand to make a lot of money. Kindly note that this cannot be practiced everywhere, and there are stringent regulations concerning forex trading. It's a highly regulated activity. You will need much knowledge and sometimes the right to operate such a system. You can contact us to learn how to trade forex.

3. Organize Events and Trainings

All the above are practical – active ways of making money. Attend the Level Up Conference for a more detailed explanation. It is a yearly limited-seat conference where ideas on how to strengthen the economic frontiers of entrepreneurial ventures are exchanged and discussed.

4. How to Establish a Passive Income

Here is an additional list of our top ten income-generating options to guide your wealth-creation efforts:

a) Save and invest in stocks, mutual funds, or treasury bills.

b) As a young graduate, it is very important to note that, aside from your field of specialization, you need to learn or improve on your ability to be a multi-diversified or multi-tasked individual at least in one or two other jobs of interest, taking into consideration your health and abilities. Some of the ways to increase one's wealth are through savings, investment in stocks, mutual fund schemes, treasury bills, etc. to save for tomorrow. This is one of the pillars of consistent investment returns.

c) Publish a book, music, or artistic work: What can you do naturally aside from your studies? I have seen many talented students who have published influential books and ended up impacting their generation. Use your talent as an income-generating venture.

d) Retail and delivery services.
e) Teaching or Organizing of Events: Free or paid.
f) Article writing, Editing, or Ghostwriting.
g) Perform household services.
h) Transport and Courier Services.
i) Horticulture or Gardening.
j) Animal Rearing.

Most graduates nowadays eschew some of these ventures due to their predisposition, but undoubtedly individuals who are into these ventures are excelling a great deal. A recent example is the tilapia business, poultry farming, etc.

Mhlongo-Ngwenya suggests starting with what you have. 'A graduate entering the workplace will not readily obtain a board membership, but they could capitalize on the growingly lucrative social media marketing industry to generate income. Choosing the right income strategy will be determined by your skill set, time capacity, existing resources, existing capital, and network of people.

In summary, the "right" income strategy is the one you can capitalize on without losing any current assets you have and one that you can embark on immediately. All the above are some of the major places and avenues where serious-minded individuals can harness and make it in life. Carefully assess yourself and identify the areas that will add value and increase your financial standing. Due to the global economic crunch, one's salary may not be enough, but learning or investing in one of these sectors or areas could be beneficial and rewarding.

I trust that this short piece has been of immense blessing and help to you. See you at the top. Best Wishes.

About
LUP CONSULT LTD

Lupconsult Limited – An Advisory Chamber for Capacity Development of individuals – HCD and organizations – ICD in Ghana and West Africa. We believe that the engine growth of every emerging economy is a well-trained labour force and strategically empowered and resourced organisation.

Mission Statement

To provide a healthy and innovative, practical stimulating experience for institutions, individuals, and students to maximize their potential, develop critical thinking skills, and become leaders in their respective field of endeavour.

Vision Statement

An established high-performance and innovative labour force and institution for economic growth and development.

Our Core Values

- Partnerships through meaningful collaboration
- Perseverance through hard work and innovation
- Integrity with honesty and at the core is trust
- Ambition with zeal to achieve – result driven
- Conscientiousness with obsessive efforts

Company Services

As a Company, we are, in all earnestness, committed

to a transformative and highly motivated labour force. All our services are need driven and directly related to helping individuals appreciate their worth and self-actualize.

1. **Career Ready:** We aim to bridge the gap between colleges and the job market. We train, connect and help individuals and young graduates to be ready for their career ambitions. Under this service, we organize
    - Internships and Volunteering opportunities
    - CV and cover letter writing and reviews
    - Boot camps for job trainings and interviews

2. **Career Direct:** This service focuses on helping our clients find their unique path to career success. Understanding and knowing oneself is the key to a satisfied career ambition.
    - Professional Development
    - Career guidance and counselling services
    - Leadership and Mentorship

3. **College Aid:** This is a study abroad initiative. Under this service, we encourage, assist and motivate individuals who wish to study abroad with meritorious scholarships and also work abroad. We also help prospective students plan financially to enable them to achieve their desire to study abroad. Professional Development, Career guidance and counselling services Leadership and Mentorship.

4. **Training & Development:** Igniting innovation and creativity for higher performance. We train individuals, corporations, and institutions with modernized technologies and skills geared towards increasing productivity and

efficiency
- Conferences and Boot Camps
- Partnerships and Exchange programmes
- Online and offline, in-person training programmes

2. **Explore Global:** We assist individuals who wish to travel to any part of the world with ease.
- Work Abroad
- Visa Acquisition/ Extensions
- Educational Tourisms.

Target Group / Fields
- State and Private Institutions
- Students/Graduate/Newly employed officers
- Educational Institutions
- Media and Entertainment Circles
- Religious Bodies

Become A Partner Today!

Many Organisations and individuals have contacted us about partnerships and sponsorships. We thought it would be great to once again open this opportunity to people who believe in this project. If you are led to donate or be a partner to ensure this idea gets realized, kindly email lupconsult20@gmail.com.

Kindly make the subject of your email, Partnership/Donation. You can also call us at +233546830029. These donations will be used to assist and help youths and students who have almost given up on life and are at a crossroads in choosing a career. This is what the *CAREER LIFE CAMPAIGN* is all about.

References

1. Career Planning. (n.d.). *Action Plan*. Retrieved from http://careerplanning.about.com/cs/actionplans/a/action_plan.htm
2. Investing Value. (n.d.). Retrieved from http://www.investingvalue.com
3. Koranteng-Pipim, S., & Aryee, J. R. (2012). *The transformed mind*. Michigan: Eaglesonline Books.
4. Ocran, A., & Ocran, C. (2015). *Career starter pack*. Ghana: Combert Impression.
5. Quarm, B. (2017). *Career nugget*. Accra: Brandsoft Studio.
6. EnCampuss. (n.d.). Retrieved from http://www.encampuss.com